RESONANT RICHES

How to Reclaim and Align Your Wealth Frequency for Abundance

Alden Gray

Table of Contents

Introduction	1
I'd Love to Hear From You!	4
Author Biography	5
Biography	5
Chapter 1	6
Understanding Energy: The Foundation of Reality	6
The Quantum Physics Perspective on Energy and Matter	7
How Thoughts and Emotions Influence Energy Vibrations	10
Final Insights	13
Chapter 2	14
Tuning into Wealth Frequencies	14
Practical Techniques for Adjusting Energetic Frequency	15
Scientific Principles Behind Frequency Tuning	17
Summary and Reflections	20
Chapter 3	22
Harnessing the Power of Sound Frequencies	22
The Influence of 528 Hz on Transformation and Wealth Attraction	23
Case Studies of Frequency Application in Manifestation	26
Insights	28
Chapter 4	29
Mindfulness and Meditation for Financial Prosperity	29
Meditation Techniques for Financial Abundance	30
Mindfulness Strategies for Overcoming Financial Blocks	33
Closing Remarks	36
Chapter 5	38
Overcoming Financial Blocks	38
Techniques for Releasing Resistance to Wealth	39
The Importance of Reframing Financial Setbacks	42
Thoughts	44
Chapter 6	46
Reprogramming the Subconscious Mind	46
Visualization Techniques for Wealth Mindset	47
Harnessing Affirmations for Financial Prosperity	50

Concluding Thoughts	52
Chapter 7	54
Maintaining Alignment with the Wealth Frequency	54
Long-term Strategies to Stay Connected to Abundance	55
Monitoring Personal Energy Levels and Making Adjustments	58
Thoughts	60
Chapter 8	62
Integrating Spiritual Wisdom with Practical Finance	62
Balancing Metaphysical Principles with Real-World Finance	63
Creating a Holistic Financial Plan Using Spiritual Tools	66
Concluding Thoughts	68
Chapter 9	70
The Gateway to Wealth Consciousness	70
The Gateway Process and the Frequency of Wealth	70
Jacobo Grinberg and the Consciousness Field of Wealth	71
Neville Goddard and the Power of Imaginal Wealth	72
Jiddu Krishnamurti and the Observer's Liberation from Lack	73
Closing Reflection: Your Inner Gateway Has Always Been There	75
Chapter 10	76
Mastering Your Personal Wealth Gateway	76
From Understanding to Embodiment	76
Clearing Subconscious Resistance and Limiting Beliefs	78
Energy Expansion Practice (Gateway Field Exercise):	79
Advanced Reality Creation—A Wealth Gateway Ritual	79
Final Reflection: You Are the Gateway	82
Now live as if your wealth is already here—because in the quantum realm of consciousness...it is!	83
Conclusion	84
I'd Love to Hear From You!	87

Introduction

What if you could tap into the power of the universe to improve your financial situation? This book invites you into a fascinating exploration where money is not merely a means to an end but a dynamic, living energy that interacts with the vibrational essence of who you are. Imagine stepping into a world where wealth flows into your life as naturally as a river follows its course—where the barriers between you and abundance dissolve simply by harmonizing the invisible frequencies of your being.

At the heart of this journey is understanding that everything around and within us is composed of energy. From the chair you sit in to the thoughts racing through your mind, every entity vibrates at its own unique frequency. Just like a skilled musician who tunes their instrument for a perfect melody, you too can attune your personal energy to resonate with the frequencies of prosperity.

Take a moment to reflect on your experiences with money. Have there been times when it felt like a smooth ride, only to transform abruptly into a rocky road full of challenges? These cyclical patterns aren't mere coincidences or isolated events; they are reflections of the energetic states we find ourselves in. The good news is that these patterns can shift. By coming to terms with how your personal vibrations align—or misalign—with the frequency of financial abundance, you open up new pathways for transformation.

One powerful gateway to this transformation is the 528 Hz frequency. Known as the "miracle tone," this specific vibration has been praised for its ability to foster healing and facilitate profound shifts in consciousness. By tuning yourself to this frequency, you create a resonance that can unlock doors to financial success previously believed to be immovable. In this book, we'll dive deep into what makes 528 Hz a cornerstone for attracting wealth and well-being, offering you a practical tool to incorporate into your daily life.

We are about to embark on an enlightening expedition together, one that transcends traditional notions of money management and dives deeper into the art of manifesting wealth through energy alignment. Whether you're a seasoned practitioner of mindfulness techniques, a spiritual seeker eager to merge metaphysical insights with material gains, or someone curious about integrating scientific principles into manifestation practices, this book offers you valuable insights tailored to your journey.

As we progress through the chapters, you'll discover various methods to align your vibrational frequency with that of financial abundance, effectively navigating and dismantling inner blocks that may have held you back. We will explore scientifically-backed strategies alongside ancient wisdom, creating a harmonious blend of old and new that speaks directly to the holistic nature of true wealth creation.

Prepare yourself for a transformational adventure. You'll be equipped with tools and techniques to attune your personal energy, navigate financial hurdles, and ultimately reshape your reality into one of sustainable abundance. From mindfulness exercises to energy healing practices, we'll cover a wide array of topics designed to elevate your financial consciousness.

Throughout this book, real-life stories and examples will illustrate the highs and lows of financial journeys and showcase how individuals from all walks of life have successfully aligned their energies to attract greater prosperity. These narratives serve as reminders that the possibilities of unlocking abundance are accessible to everyone, regardless of their starting point.

As you delve into each chapter, consider this text not just as a guide, but as a companion on your path toward a more fulfilling financial existence. This is not a one-size-fits-all solution but rather a customizable framework that honors the uniqueness of your individual journey. You are encouraged to adopt the ideas and practices that resonate with you, adjust them to fit your lifestyle, and witness firsthand the transformations that will unfold.

So, get ready to redefine your relationship with money. Let go of any preconceived notions that limit your potential and embrace the idea that wealth is not an elusive goal but an experience waiting to be realized through the subtle yet potent language of energy. Together, we'll illuminate the steps necessary to cultivate a rich, abundant life, deeply interwoven with the vibrant tapestry of the universe.

Join me on this mesmerizing journey where science meets spirituality, and prosperity becomes a natural extension of your being. As you read on, I encourage you to keep an open heart and mind, allowing curiosity and wonder to guide your learning process. May this exploration inspire you to reclaim your innate capacity for wealth and abundance, turning dreams into tangible realities. Welcome to a new paradigm of financial freedom, where the power to thrive lies authentically within you.

I'D LOVE TO HEAR FROM YOU!

If *Resonate With Riches* sparked a shift in your mindset, offered you clarity, or helped you align with the abundance you've always deserved—your feedback would mean the world to me.

Your honest review not only supports my journey as an author, but it also helps fellow readers discover this book at the perfect moment in their own lives. Even just a few words can make a powerful difference.

Please take a minute to leave a review on Amazon or Goodreads.
It helps more than you know—and I read every single one with deep gratitude.

With heartfelt thanks,
Alden Gray

Author Biography

Biography

Alden Gray is a seasoned author, spiritual guide, and retired entrepreneur based in Bangkok. Born in Hong Kong and now 60 years old, Alden has over 35 years of mastery in Taoism, meditation, and mind force, dedicating his life to exploring the intricate connections between energy, manifestation, and the flow of wealth. After a successful business career, he transitioned to a path of deep spiritual discovery, including a transformative period as a short-term monk in Thailand. Alden's writing uniquely blends practical wisdom from his entrepreneurial background with profound spiritual insights gained from his experiences in Taoism and Buddhism. His work offers readers a compelling journey into the power of frequency, vibration, and universal laws to unlock personal abundance, inner harmony, and life transformation. His major works include "Guardians of the Mystic Dragon," "Shadows Over the Enchanted Academy," "Guardians of the Time Balance," "Guardians of Destiny," "What is the Cost of Truth in a Galaxy of Lies," and "Unraveling the Multiverse," showcasing themes of magic, cosmic balance, and the complexities of truth and duty in both Sci-Fi and fantasy genres. Self-published across platforms like KDP, Kobo, and Google Partner, Alden continues to inspire others from his home in Bangkok through his writings and active engagement on three YouTube channels.

Chapter 1

Understanding Energy: The Foundation of Reality

Understanding energy is like unlocking the secrets of how our universe functions, where everything from the air we breathe to the money we spend is a part of this energetic tapestry. Energy isn't just an abstract concept presented in science textbooks; it's the essence that connects all things, vibrating at unique frequencies that define their nature. For many, the idea that money is also energy might seem far-fetched, yet this perspective opens up a world of possibilities for those who dare to explore it. This chapter aims to bridge the gap between what we perceive as reality and the less tangible properties that govern it through the lens of quantum physics. It's an invitation to rethink how we view wealth, encouraging a shift from traditional beliefs to a more dynamic understanding of financial empowerment. By grasping these concepts, one can begin to see money not just as a physical currency but as an integral part of a grander energetic cycle.

In this enlightening journey, readers will delve into a variety of subjects, starting with the fascinating relationship between energy and matter as understood through quantum physics. The chapter will break down how this scientific framework challenges what we consider tangible and showcases the potential for interconnectedness at a fundamental level. Discussions will then transition into how these principles apply to the concept of money, offering insights into how aligning with its frequency can transform one's approach to wealth building. From practical strategies like visualization and affirmations to exploring emotional states that influence financial outcomes, the chapter offers actionable advice for tapping into the vibrational flow of abundance. Whether you're curious about mindfulness practices or interested in integrating metaphysical principles into your financial life, the content promises to provide a rich amalgam of ideas designed to inspire and empower. Engaging with these insights could lead to transformational shifts in both personal growth and financial well-being, making the quest for prosperity an enlightening adventure filled with new opportunities and profound realizations.

THE QUANTUM PHYSICS PERSPECTIVE ON ENERGY AND MATTER

In the realm of quantum physics, the distinction between energy and matter is not as clear-cut as we might traditionally perceive. This groundbreaking science reveals that at a fundamental level, all that exists in our universe, right down to solid objects, is composed of vibrating energy fields—or quanta. This notion challenges the conventional understanding of reality being purely physical. Through this lens, everything is interconnected through these energetic vibrations, suggesting an intricate web of interaction far beyond our everyday perception.

This interconnectedness has profound implications for how we view money. Traditionally, money is seen primarily as physical currency or digits on a screen—tangible assets we use to exchange goods and services. However, if we apply quantum physics principles, money becomes more than just a physical entity. It transforms into a manifestation of energy, resonating at specific frequencies like everything else in the universe. This perspective shifts the paradigm, emphasizing that wealth can be attracted and influenced by aligning with its vibrational frequency.

Recognizing money as energy encourages us to adopt a mindset focused on financial abundance. When we understand that both wealth and poverty operate on certain frequencies, it becomes possible to consciously engage with these energies. This awareness motivates a shift from viewing money as a scarce resource to seeing it as a form of energy we can attract by aligning our own frequencies with those of wealth. For instance, adopting positive affirmations, expressing gratitude for what you have, and visualizing financial goals are practical ways to enhance one's vibrational alignment with abundance.

The concept of vibrational frequency also serves as a powerful metaphor for personal growth and financial empowerment. Just as a radio tunes into different stations by adjusting frequency, individuals can elevate their vibration to align with opportunities for financial growth. This involves cultivating thoughts, emotions, and actions that resonate with high-frequency states such as joy, love, and abundance. By doing so, one positions themselves to not only attract prosperity but also to recognize and seize opportunities when they arise.

Understanding the vibrational frequency of wealth encourages a holistic approach to financial success. It suggests that boosting one's energy frequency isn't merely about accumulating more money but also involves developing a prosperous mindset. This involves integrating mindfulness practices, fostering a positive outlook on financial matters, and engaging in energy healing techniques to remove any blocks hindering one's financial flow. Such practices help individuals remain open and receptive to the flow of wealth, ensuring that energy moves freely rather than stagnates or dissipates.

As quantum physics shows that subatomic particles exist in a state of potential until observed, we can draw parallels to our financial realities. The idea that our attention can influence outcome supports the belief that focusing on financial goals can actualize prosperity. By directing mental energy towards desired financial outcomes—whether it's securing a new job, growing a business, or investing wisely—we begin to shape our material world.

To effectively utilize these insights, individuals should consider guidelines for tuning into higher frequencies. First, practice mindful awareness of your current energy state and how it relates to money. Acknowledge any limiting beliefs or negative attitudes toward wealth and actively seek to transform them. Next, engage in daily rituals that raise your vibrational frequency, such as meditation, gratitude exercises, and visualization techniques. Lastly, stay open to synchronicities and unexpected opportunities for financial gain; these are often signs that you are aligned with the energy of abundance.

How Thoughts and Emotions Influence Energy Vibrations

In the pursuit of financial empowerment, many have turned their attention towards understanding how our internal states—our thoughts and emotions—play a crucial role in shaping the financial opportunities that come our way. At its core, this idea hinges on the principle that everything vibrates at specific frequencies, including our feelings and mental focus. By aligning these vibrations with those of wealth and abundance, we can significantly influence our financial landscape.

To begin with, it is helpful to understand how feelings resonate at specific frequencies. Our emotions, such as joy, gratitude, and confidence, emit high-frequency vibrations, while negative emotions like fear, anxiety, and guilt tend to vibrate at lower frequencies. This dynamic affects what we attract into our lives. For instance, when you are filled with positive feelings about money, you align yourself with similar energies, thereby increasing the likelihood of attracting financial abundance. Think of it as tuning into a radio station; your emotional state is the dial, and by turning it towards positivity, you receive clearer signals from the universe to attract wealth.

Clear and focused thoughts are another key element in enhancing our vibrational resonance with wealth energy. The power of having a well-defined goal cannot be understated. When you have clarity in your financial aspirations, you amplify the signal you send out, making it easier for wealth-related opportunities to find their way to you. It's much like setting a GPS for a specific destination. With a clear address entered, you can chart a more direct and efficient path. Similarly, when your financial goals are vividly imagined and kept at the forefront of your mind, they become more tangible and achievable.

The Law of Attraction, a well-discussed concept in both spiritual and financial circles, plays an integral role here. At its essence, the law suggests that like attracts like. By consciously aligning your thoughts and emotions with prosperity, you draw in opportunities that match your vibrational output. Visualization and affirmations are practical tools that help reinforce this alignment. Regularly envisioning yourself achieving financial success can shift your subconscious beliefs, breaking down any mental barriers to wealth. A simple yet powerful exercise involves writing down daily affirmations, such as "I am open to receiving infinite financial resources," and reflecting on them through meditation or journaling.

Furthermore, it's important to acknowledge the holistic nature of financial prosperity. Our mental and emotional states don't just exist in isolation; they also have profound effects on our physical realities. Often, individuals who experience significant financial growth report not only changes in their bank accounts but also transformations in their overall health and relationships. This interconnection underscores the necessity of a balanced approach to prosperity. By nurturing your mind, body, and spirit, you create a fertile ground for financial seeds to grow.

Guidelines for cultivating these beneficial vibrations can be immensely valuable. First, practice mindfulness to become acutely aware of your thoughts and emotions. Paying attention to your internal dialogue helps you identify patterns that may hinder your financial well-being. Distinguishing between constructive and destructive thought patterns allows you to consciously choose higher-frequency thoughts aligned with abundance. Second, foster a supportive environment by surrounding yourself with people who share your vision for prosperity. Engaging with communities that reinforce positive perspectives and celebrate success can exponentially elevate your vibrational frequency.

Additionally, consider the impacts of gratitude and giving. By regularly expressing gratitude for what you currently possess, you enhance the vibrational pull towards acquiring more. It shifts your focus from lack to appreciation, opening up new channels for financial flow. Similarly, practicing generosity by giving back—whether through time, resources, or knowledge—not only enriches others but also multiplies your own abundance. What you put forth into the world often returns tenfold, reinforcing the energy cycle of receiving and sharing.

Ultimately, awareness and intentionality are paramount. Reflect on moments when you felt most financially empowered and examine the underlying feelings and thoughts during those times. Was it confidence? Determination? An unwavering belief in your capability to generate wealth? Use these insights as a blueprint for crafting your current and future financial trajectory.

Final Insights

Throughout this chapter, we've delved into the idea that everything in our universe, including money, is an expression of energy vibrating at different frequencies. We've examined how quantum physics reveals this interconnectedness and how it reshapes our understanding of wealth. Money isn't just something physical; it's an energetic presence that can be attracted by aligning with its frequency. By seeing money as a form of energy, we open ourselves to greater financial possibilities and empowerment. This shift in perspective encourages us to focus on cultivating thoughts and emotions that resonate with prosperity, effectively tuning into a universal frequency that supports financial growth.

As you move forward, embracing these concepts can transform how you approach wealth and abundance. It's about more than just accumulating funds—it's about fostering a mindset that aligns with positive vibrations. Incorporating practices like mindfulness, gratitude, and visualization can elevate your vibrational state, making it easier to attract opportunities for prosperity. Reflecting on personal experiences where you felt financially empowered can provide insights into replicating those feelings and thoughts. By doing so, you create a blueprint for achieving future goals and realize the profound potential that comes from harmonizing with the energy of abundance.

Chapter 2

Tuning into Wealth Frequencies

Tuning into wealth frequencies is an intriguing journey that merges the power of personal energy alignment with financial success. Imagine living a life where your thoughts, emotions, and intentions vibrate at the same frequency as abundance itself. This chapter invites you to explore how the energy you emit can influence the wealth you attract. It's not just about envisioning prosperity; it's about creating a lifestyle that aligns every fiber of your being with the frequencies of wealth. By understanding this connection, you open the door to transformative experiences that go beyond mere financial gain to enhance well-being and fulfillment.

Throughout this chapter, you'll delve into practical techniques designed to fine-tune your personal frequency toward wealth attraction. We'll guide you through meditative practices, illustrating how visualization during these sessions can lay the foundation for financial prosperity by drawing detailed blueprints of your dreams. You'll also discover the possibilities of sound therapy and learn how specific frequencies can unlock new levels of consciousness conducive to wealth resonance. Coupled with the power of affirmations, these methods help reprogram your subconscious beliefs about money, making wealth attraction feel both natural and achievable. Additionally, we'll explore energetic cleansing rituals that remove emotional blockages, ensuring unhindered pathways for abundance to flow into your life. Finally, backed by scientific principles, you'll gain insight into how tuning into these frequencies is not just mystical but rooted in empirical evidence, providing actionable strategies for your journey to financial empowerment.

Practical Techniques for Adjusting Energetic Frequency

In our journey to recalibrate energetic frequency for wealth, meditative practices serve as a fundamental tool. Imagine using guided meditations not just to relax, but to transform your mindset towards financial prosperity. When engaged regularly, these sessions allow you to delve deeply into personal energy fields, making it possible to visualize and attract abundance actively. Picture yourself in a serene space, eyes closed, gradually quieting the inner chatter that's often filled with doubts about money. As you do this, envision an influx of prosperity entering your life, erasing scarcity and planting seeds of abundance in its place.

The power of visualization during meditation cannot be overstated. It is akin to drafting the blueprint of your financial dreams before constructing them in reality. This practice helps to calm the mind, creating a fertile ground for new thoughts and ideas about wealth that are more aligned with abundance. It's not just about quietude; it's about cultivating a receptive mental state where wealth-building ideas can germinate and flourish.

Moving forward, sound therapy offers another engaging approach to align personal frequency with wealth. By integrating specific sound frequencies, individuals can break through their limiting beliefs and open themselves up to deeper experiences of wealth resonance. These sonic vibrations have been empirically shown to influence brain wave patterns, promoting states of consciousness that are conducive to manifestation and prosperity enhancement.

When you listen to these frequencies, think of them as a bridge between your current financial state and the abundant future you aim to create. The vibrations work their way through your subconscious barriers, shifting your perceptions and energizing your intentions. Tailoring your experiences with different soundscapes or instruments may deepen your wealth resonance, as each individual's energetic makeup interacts uniquely with various frequencies.

Affirmation practices enhance this journey by reprogramming subconscious beliefs surrounding money. Crafting affirmations isn't simply about writing down words; it's about creating powerful statements that resonate with your emotional state and desired self-worth. When you regularly state these affirmations with conviction—"I am deserving of wealth," "Money flows to me easily"—you begin to condition your mind to perceive these claims as truths.

Linking affirmations to emotional states is crucial. For instance, while saying "I am financially successful," connect it with feelings of joy and gratitude as if your affirmation were already a reality. This potentiates the law of attraction by aligning thought (the affirmation) with emotion (feeling) and catalyzing the manifestation process. It's about turning abstract desires into concrete realities through consistent, focused intention.

Energetic cleansing presents yet another potent strategy in tuning into wealth frequencies. Cleansing rituals, such as smudging with sage or employing crystals like citrine or pyrite, serve to eliminate emotional blockages tied to money and protect against stagnation. These practices cleanse both the physical and energetic space, enhancing clarity and openness to financial prospects.

As you engage in these rituals, envision the smoke from smudging enveloping and dissolving any monetary anxieties or fears you hold. See it clearing out all stagnant energy, leaving a harmonious environment conducive to wealth creation. Crystals, too, offer support; when used strategically, they act as amplifiers of financial frequency connection, elevating one's energetic signature to resonate more closely with abundance.

Such cleansing does more than just purify; it creates a vibrant canvas upon which new financial patterns and opportunities can manifest. Regularly incorporating these rituals into your routine ensures that your energetic channels remain unobstructed, allowing wealth to find its way to you without hinderance.

Scientific Principles Behind Frequency Tuning

The concept of tuning into wealth frequencies may sound mystical, but it rests on a robust scientific foundation that can have tangible impacts on financial outcomes. The essence of this idea is that everything in the universe operates at a specific frequency—including our thoughts and emotions—and by adjusting these frequencies, individuals can create opportunities for increased prosperity and abundance. Understanding how frequency works universally helps inspire conscious wealth-attracting efforts, guiding readers to recognize their own money vibrations.

Frequency serves as an invisible thread connecting every aspect of life. When you understand the vibrational frequency of different energies, you unlock the potential to consciously attract wealth. For instance, consider the changes in technology when shifted from analog to digital; the underlying shift was essentially a change in frequency. Similarly, in personal development, raising your vibrational state can translate to aligning with frequencies that draw wealth. Once you identify your current money vibrations, which might be influenced by past experiences or learned behaviors, you can work on elevating them. This conscious recognition and adjustment become empowering tools that promote financial growth.

A fascinating area related to frequency is bioenergetics, which deals with the flow of energy through living systems. Each person has a unique energy matrix that influences their physical, mental, and financial health. By engaging with and understanding this personal energy field, individuals can make intentional adjustments to attract wealth. Imagine your energy matrix as a complex web, each strand vibrating with its frequency. When you nurture positivity and focus on wealth-enhancing thoughts, this web begins resonating differently, attracting similar positive frequencies from the world.

For example, practices like tai chi or yoga are renowned for aligning one's internal energy, creating harmony that can extend to financial well-being. By learning to navigate and influence your bioenergy, you position yourself strategically to enhance both physical vitality and financial success.

Moving forward, the intersection of neuroscience with wealth attraction reveals compelling insights into how our brains function in relation to abundance. Neuroscience shows us that our thought patterns shape our neural pathways, which in turn can significantly impact our financial behavior. Scarcity mindsets, often deeply ingrained through repeated negative experiences, can lead to neurological patterns that inhibit financial progress. However, due to neuroplasticity—the brain's ability to rewire itself—it's possible to transform these scarcity-linked pathways into ones conducive to wealth thinking. For instance, if regular meditation or mindfulness practices encourage noticing abundance in daily life, they help in establishing new neural routes that foster gratitude and attract prosperity over time. Such deliberate practice in recognizing and reshaping thoughts not only broadens personal perception but also aligns neural frequencies toward abundance.

Real-world validation of frequency tuning's efficacy emerges through empirical evidence. Several studies have linked frequency work to enhanced prosperity-building practices, providing compelling illustrations of frequency's role in financial success. In one study, practitioners who regularly engaged in vibration-raising exercises, such as mantras or energy healing, reported significant improvements in both mindset and material circumstances. Their results offer encouraging evidence that incorporating tuning practices into daily routines leads to substantial benefits. Another research from institutes focused on psychological well-being has demonstrated that individuals practicing techniques to alter their vibrational states experienced greater satisfaction and financial stability compared to control groups not engaged in such practices. These findings underscore the real-world impact of frequency work and advocate for daily practice integration.

Tuning into wealth frequencies, then, becomes less about abstract theories and more about practical, scientifically-backed strategies to improve financial outcomes. By embracing these concepts—understanding frequency, navigating our bioenergetic fields, harnessing neuroscience insights, and acknowledging empirical evidence—we lay a solid foundation for attracting prosperity. Each element provides unique insights: from identifying and adjusting our vibrational signatures to rewiring our minds for abundance, and ultimately adopting practices validated by science to ensure we resonate with wealth.

SUMMARY AND REFLECTIONS

In this chapter, we've explored a variety of techniques to adjust your personal frequency and align it with wealth. From meditation and visualization to sound therapy and affirmation practices, each method offers a unique pathway to amplify your energetic vibration. By integrating these practices into daily life, you open yourself up to new possibilities of prosperity. It's more than just following steps; it's about creating a mindset that's ready to receive abundance. By tapping into the power of these techniques, you're not only fostering a sense of financial wellbeing but also transforming your overall approach to wealth creation.

Understanding the scientific underpinnings reinforces the validity of tuning into wealth frequencies. Concepts like bioenergetics and neuroscience provide a backdrop to how our thoughts and energetic fields can shape financial success. The real-world evidence underscores that these aren't mere theories—incorporating these practices offers tangible benefits. As you continue on this journey, remember that aligning your energy with abundance is an empowering step towards attaining the financial freedom you seek. Embrace these strategies with an open mind and watch as they help manifest the wealth and prosperity you've envisioned for yourself.

Chapter 3

Harnessing the Power of Sound Frequencies

Exploring the world of sound frequencies opens a fascinating pathway to understanding how specific vibrations can influence our perceptions and attract wealth. It's intriguing how these frequencies, particularly the 528 Hz, often referred to as the 'Love frequency,' offer more than just calming sounds; they present an opportunity to transform one's mindset about money and abundance. Imagine tuning into a frequency that helps realign your beliefs from scarcity to abundance, inviting prosperity through a shift in consciousness. In a world where financial empowerment is sought after, the potential of aligning with this powerful sound cannot be understated. By inviting this vibrational harmony into daily life, individuals are encouraged to unlock doors toward holistic wealth consciousness, all by simply engaging with the magic of sound.

In this chapter, we'll delve into how the 528 Hz frequency uniquely positions itself as a tool for financial transformation, providing a fresh perspective on wealth attraction. You'll discover practical guidelines and strategies to integrate this frequency into your everyday routine, enhancing your financial beliefs and resisting traditional constraints. The chapter will explore scientific research supporting the efficacy of sound frequencies in fostering neural changes that empower transformative thinking about money. Additionally, you'll uncover inspiring stories and case studies where individuals have effectively harnessed the power of 528 Hz to reshape their economic experiences and attract opportunities. By the end, you'll have a comprehensive understanding of how to incorporate this seemingly mystical element of sound into both spiritual and financial practices, encouraging shifts in perception needed to pursue wealth with renewed energy and confidence.

THE INFLUENCE OF 528 HZ ON TRANSFORMATION AND WEALTH ATTRACTION

In the realm of sound frequencies, 528 Hz holds a special place as the 'Love frequency,' renowned for its ability to heal and transform. Harnessing this particular frequency can lead to profound shifts in consciousness, aligning beliefs with abundance and wealth. For many seeking a deeper understanding of sound frequency's power, it offers an alternative approach to traditional financial strategies, inviting individuals on a journey toward holistic wealth consciousness.

The magic of 528 Hz begins with its inherent ability to foster deep emotional healing. As the Love frequency, it resonates at a vibration that encourages positivity, opening gateways to elevate thoughts and attitudes. This transformation isn't just a shift in perception; it's a tangible change in energy that aligns personal beliefs with the vibrations of abundance. When individuals regularly immerse themselves in this frequency, they find their mental landscape conducive to prosperity—

perceptions begin to shift, and old, limiting patterns dissolve.

Regular exposure to 528 Hz can be likened to watering a plant—the more it's nurtured, the better it flourishes. Listening to this sound frequency consistently allows the subconscious mind to absorb positive financial beliefs. By bathing the subconscious in these harmonious tones, barriers are dismantled, paving the way for new empowering narratives around money and success. It's akin to reprogramming a computer; outdated software is replaced with efficient new codes designed to enhance performance.

Guidelines for incorporating 528 Hz into daily life can provide structure and enhance its impact on financial beliefs. One might consider starting each day with a brief listening session of 528 Hz music, setting a tone of optimism and openness. Additionally, creating a ritualistic atmosphere where this frequency plays softly in the background during daily activities can encourage a constant state of receptivity. Such practices gently push aside negative thoughts related to scarcity, allowing new, prosperous ideas to take root.

Beyond passive listening, intentional engagement with 528 Hz during meditation or planning sessions can amplify its benefits. When the mind is stilled and focused, it reaches a state of heightened awareness, making it fertile ground for significant mindset shifts. By weaving 528 Hz into meditative practices, individuals cultivate a profound relaxation that also serves as a gateway to clearer vision and goal-setting concerning wealth. During these moments of quiet reflection, creativity flows unhindered, encouraging a natural connection to the energies of wellness and prosperity.

The practice of pairing affirmations with this sound frequency further anchors intention, solidifying one's commitment to a wealth-conscious lifestyle. Affirmations act as powerful declarations of self-belief and purpose, carving pathways for goals manifest into reality. When spoken over the soothing backdrop of 528 Hz, these affirmations carry additional weight, using sound as a medium to embed convictions into one's psyche. This sound-as-catalyst approach makes abstract concepts of wealth and abundance feel more attainable and grounded in everyday life.

As we explore the role of 528 Hz in nurturing wealth consciousness, it's essential to recognize that its effects extend beyond mere theory. Scientific insights suggest that our brains respond dynamically to sound frequencies, with certain notes fostering neural plasticity —our brain's ability to reorganize itself by forming new neural connections. In the context of financial empowerment, this means people have the capacity to reshape how they perceive money, pivoting from fear and uncertainty to hope and assurance.

To maximize the benefits of 528 Hz, individuals can integrate specific guidelines into their spiritual and financial routines. Engaging with this frequency should be viewed as both a personal exploration and a disciplined practice. Establishing consistency is key; much like any transformative endeavor, it requires dedication and patience. Setting aside dedicated moments—whether in the morning or before sleep—to consciously listen and resonate with 528 Hz helps reinforce the mental and emotional shifts necessary for lasting change.

CASE STUDIES OF FREQUENCY APPLICATION IN MANIFESTATION

The power of sound frequencies, especially the 528 Hz frequency, has emerged as a remarkable tool for transforming financial reality. This concept has found its way into the routines of individuals who have witnessed significant positive changes in their income and opportunities. Take, for instance, a story of an entrepreneur who incorporated the 528 Hz frequency into her daily life. By listening to this frequency during her morning routine, she reported experiencing newfound clarity and heightened creativity, which helped her land lucrative deals and expand her business network. This demonstrates that the integration of sound frequencies can align one's energy with the vibration of abundance, thus opening doors to wealth generation.

Scientific research supports these anecdotal observations by highlighting measurable physiological changes when exposed to the 528 Hz frequency. Studies suggest that this frequency can alter brainwave patterns, promoting a state conducive to transformative thinking about money consciousness. The implications are profound; by stimulating neuroplasticity, individuals can rewire limiting beliefs and attitudes toward wealth. Such exposure has been linked to a more optimistic outlook on financial prospects, fostering a readiness to pursue new opportunities and embrace risks with greater confidence.

Experiments conducted in group settings further unveil the potential of sound frequencies in enhancing wealth consciousness. Sound healing sessions and visualization workshops create environments where individuals report feeling a collective shift in perception about financial well-being. In such gatherings, participants are encouraged to visualize their financial goals while immersed in the sounds of the 528 Hz frequency. This practice magnifies not only personal empowerment but also community support. The resulting sense of unity and shared purpose catalyzes shifts in individual attitudes towards money, encouraging actions aligned with increased prosperity.

Overcoming skepticism is crucial in embracing sound frequencies as tools for financial transformation. Many hold tightly to conventional views of wealth accumulation that may not recognize the benefits of alternative approaches like sound healing. Addressing these doubts requires presenting evidence-based practices and stories of personal success. Acknowledging the fears associated with unconventional methods while highlighting the science behind sound frequencies can bolster open-mindedness. Engaging skeptics involves offering strategies that gradually integrate sound into financial planning, proving its merit without dismissing traditional viewpoints.

Integrating affirmations and intention-setting with sound frequencies enhances their impact. Affirmations paired with 528 Hz frequencies act as potent catalysts, fortifying positive mental frameworks that attract abundance. Implementing these practices involves choosing specific affirmations that resonate personally and consistently using them alongside sound therapy. For instance, setting a daily intention such as "I am worthy of financial success" during moments spent with 528 Hz music can deepen the listener's connection to prosperity consciousness. These guidelines become instrumental as they help embed new beliefs at both conscious and unconscious levels.

Insights

As we wrap up our discussion on the transformative power of 528 Hz, it's clear that this sound frequency offers more than just a unique listening experience. It serves as a bridge between traditional financial practices and holistic approaches to wealth consciousness. By tuning into this frequency, you open yourself up to new thought patterns that foster abundance. The simple practice of listening to 528 Hz can gradually shift your mindset from scarcity to prosperity, helping you align with the vibrations of abundance in your everyday life.

We've seen how scientific research backs these claims, showing that certain sound frequencies can encourage positive changes in the brain. This isn't just theoretical; real-life examples demonstrate how incorporating 528 Hz into daily routines has led to significant improvements in people's relationships with money. Whether you're just starting to explore alternative methods for financial growth or you're already immersed in spiritual practices, embracing the potential of 528 Hz can be a valuable addition to your journey towards wealth and well-being.

Chapter 4

Mindfulness and Meditation for Financial Prosperity

Harnessing the power of mindfulness and meditation can lead to financial prosperity. This chapter invites readers into a journey where ancient practices meet modern-day goals, offering a unique pathway to wealth that goes beyond traditional strategies. In a world where financial success often feels elusive, integrating mindful awareness and meditative practices provides a refreshing perspective on abundance. Through cultivating a mindset rooted in presence and gratitude, individuals can transform their relationship with money, aligning their thoughts and emotions with their deepest financial aspirations. By doing so, they unlock a potent force within themselves, capable of attracting the prosperity they seek.

In this exploration, you'll discover various techniques designed to elevate your financial consciousness. The chapter guides you through morning and evening meditations tailored for abundance, teaching you how to start and end each day with intentions grounded in wealth creation. As you delve deeper, you'll learn about the power of visualization during meditation—a tool that bridges the gap between desires and reality by engaging both mind and emotion. Moreover, the chapter introduces sound frequencies known to enhance wealth attraction, offering a sensory experience that harmonizes your energy with the universe's rhythm. Complementing these meditative practices are mindfulness strategies aimed at overcoming financial blocks. You'll explore how journaling can reveal subconscious patterns that hinder wealth, while breathing exercises provide clarity for making sound financial decisions. Affirmations become powerful allies in rewiring your mindset, fostering a mental environment ripe for opportunity and growth. Mindful spending practices further ensure that your approach to money remains intentional and aligned with your values, promoting long-term financial well-being. Each section offers practical insights, empowering you to weave these ancient principles into your everyday life, ultimately redefining what financial success means to you.

Meditation Techniques for Financial Abundance

Morning Abundance Meditation establishes a practice that can significantly elevate your financial journey. Beginning each day with morning meditation allows you to set an intention grounded in gratitude and future wealth prospects. This practice focuses your thoughts on existing and anticipated abundance, creating a fertile ground for prosperity.

Start by finding a quiet space where you can sit comfortably. Close your eyes and take a few deep breaths, inviting calmness into your space. As you settle into the meditation, turn your focus inward and reflect on the abundance already present in your life. Whether it's the comfort of having a roof over your head, relationships you cherish, or skills you possess, acknowledge these blessings with appreciation. Gratitude is not just a passive state but an active force that invites more of what you appreciate. Now, visualize your financial goals as if they are already achieved. See yourself living your ideal lifestyle, feeling the emotions associated with achieving these milestones. By aligning your emotions with your visions of success, you adjust your vibrational frequency, thereby attracting opportunities aligning with your financial ambitions.

Evening Reflective Meditation offers an essential counterpart to your morning routine. The day often brings challenges and obstacles which may hinder your mindset and block your path to wealth. This evening practice helps in identifying and releasing these limiting beliefs. Throughout the day, the subconscious mind absorbs countless messages, many of which might be counterproductive to a wealth-oriented mindset. As you sit down for an evening meditation, it's time to let go of these negative impressions.

Begin by reflecting on any limiting thoughts or beliefs that surfaced during the day. Did self-doubt creep in when considering financial decisions? Were there moments of scarcity mentality? Recognize these patterns and mentally release them, visualizing them dissolving away from your consciousness. To replace these voids, open your mind to new possibilities and opportunities for growth. Consider the successes achieved during the day, no matter how small, and anchor yourself in positive achievements. Ending your day with optimistic reflections sets a welcoming tone for potential opportunities while you sleep.

Guided Wealth Frequency Meditations bring another dimension by introducing you to specific frequencies known to enhance wealth attraction. Sounds such as 528 Hz are believed to resonate with the heartbeat of the universe, establishing harmony and balance within oneself. Listening to these frequencies during meditation can awaken your innate ability to attract abundance by synchronizing your energies with universal forces.

You can find guided meditations online or create your own playlist featuring wealth frequency sounds. As you immerse yourself into these sessions, allow the tones to wash over you, aligning your personal energy with the rhythmic pulse of abundance. These sessions assist in fine-tuning your internal vibrations, making you more receptive to the flow of prosperity. Use affirmations alongside these meditative frequencies to amplify their effect. Statements like "I am aligned with the energy of abundance" or "Prosperity flows freely into my life" reinforce the frequency's power.

Visualization Techniques during Meditation serve as significant tools in bridging the gap between dreams and reality. This process engages your mind creatively, integrating the emotional components vital for manifesting visions into existence. Visualization involves constructing vivid mental images of your financial aspirations, from specific monetary goals to broader lifestyle changes you wish to experience.

To begin, enter a relaxed state of awareness, free from the distractions of daily life. Within this calm space, vividly imagine yourself achieving your financial targets. For instance, see yourself receiving a promotion, launching a successful business, or living in your dream home. Engage all your senses—what do you see, hear, smell, or feel in this prosperous reality? The more detailed your visualization, the stronger its impact. Your brain registers these detailed scenarios as experiences, reinforcing neurological pathways associated with those feelings and outcomes. Emotional engagement solidifies this connection, so allow yourself to feel excitement, joy, and satisfaction as if these experiences are already real. Regular practice weaves these visions into the fabric of your subconscious, gradually guiding your actions towards actualizing your goals.

Mindfulness Strategies for Overcoming Financial Blocks

In our quest for financial prosperity, the power of mindfulness can often be underestimated. Mindfulness offers a unique approach to recognizing and overcoming the mental blocks that may be standing in the way of true wealth. Let's delve into some mindfulness techniques that could pave the way for not just identifying these blocks but actively dismantling them.

Mindfulness Journaling serves as a profound tool in this journey. By regularly engaging in journaling, you create a space to reflect on your thoughts and feelings about money. The key lies in its ability to uncover subconscious beliefs and patterns of self-sabotage. Imagine sitting down with your journal, free from distractions, allowing your thoughts about money, success, and abundance to flow freely. As you write, you might notice recurring themes—perhaps a fear of losing money or an underlying belief that you don't deserve wealth. Recognizing these patterns is the first step towards change. Once identified, you can consciously choose to explore their origins and question their validity, gradually replacing them with more empowering narratives.

Alongside journaling, Breathing Techniques for Financial Clarity provide an immediate way to calm the mind and enhance clarity around financial decisions. Controlled breathing exercises reduce anxiety and foster a sense of peace, which allows for clearer thinking. A simple practice involves inhaling deeply through the nose, holding the breath momentarily, and then exhaling slowly through the mouth. This rhythmic breathing not only alleviates tension but also centers your mind, making it easier to focus on the task at hand—whether it's planning a budget or evaluating investment opportunities. The clarity gained from such exercises ensures that decisions are made from a place of balance rather than emotional turmoil.

Integrating Affirmative Mindfulness Practices can significantly shift one's financial mindset. These involve using positive affirmations to counteract negative thoughts and reinforce a mindset attuned to attracting wealth. For instance, repeating affirmations like "I am open to receiving abundance" or "Prosperity flows effortlessly into my life" helps rewire the brain to focus on potential and possibilities instead of limitations. Consistency is crucial here; regularly practicing affirmations instills a sense of empowerment and aligns your thought processes with your financial goals. Over time, you'll find your mindset naturally gravitating towards opportunity and growth, setting the stage for tangible improvements in your financial well-being.

Mindful Spending Practices encourage a conscious approach to how we use money, shedding light on the energetic exchange involved in every transaction. It's about being aware not just of what you're purchasing, but why. Consider reflecting on your emotions at the point of purchase—are you buying something out of necessity, or is there an emotional trigger? Mindful spending practices invite you to pause before making any financial decisions, ensuring they align with both your values and long-term goals. When practiced regularly, this mindfulness leads to more intentional spending, reducing waste and fostering a healthier relationship with money.

By embracing these mindfulness techniques, you cultivate a deeper understanding of your own financial landscape. Each practice provides a lens through which you can examine the intricate relationship between your thoughts, emotions, and financial habits. It's a process of transformation—each mindful act building upon the last, gradually reshaping your reality to reflect the prosperity you seek.

While each technique stands powerful on its own, integrating them can amplify their effects. Mindfulness journaling can be complemented by breathing exercises, grounding your reflections in serenity. Meanwhile, incorporating affirmations within your writing or during moments of mindful spending creates synergy, reinforcing the shifts you're striving to manifest.

Consider setting aside specific times daily or weekly for these practices. Create a routine where each technique finds its place, perhaps starting with journaling in the morning to set intentions for the day, followed by breathing exercises before tackling financial tasks. Affirmations might suit your evening wind-down, embedding positive thoughts just before rest. And throughout the day, maintain awareness with mindful spending, consistently anchoring yourself to the present.

As you become more attuned to the nuances of your financial behavior, you'll likely discover new perspectives on wealth itself. The traditional metrics of success, such as salary figures or material goods, may start to dissolve, replaced by measures that resonate more deeply with personal fulfillment and security. This broadened understanding of wealth acknowledges not only what you have, but how you feel about what you have—and how you can sustain it meaningfully.

Closing Remarks

Throughout this chapter, we've delved into various mindfulness and meditation practices geared towards cultivating a wealth frequency—one that consistently invites financial prosperity. By establishing routines such as Morning Abundance Meditation and Evening Reflective Meditation, you're able to shape your thoughts and emotions to align with abundance. These practices initiate a journey where gratitude becomes a powerful tool, transforming how you perceive and manifest wealth. Incorporating guided meditations and visualization techniques further enhances this process, linking your aspirations to the rhythmic energies of the universe and helping turn dreams into reality.

Mindfulness strategies offer another layer to this transformative journey by addressing mental blocks that hinder financial growth. Through tools like journaling and breathing exercises, you can uncover subconscious patterns and foster clarity in decision-making. Affirmative mindfulness practices and mindful spending encourage a shift in perspective, aligning daily actions with long-term financial goals. By integrating these techniques, you're not only fostering a richer relationship with money but also redefining what true wealth means to you. As you continue to practice these methods, remember that each step builds upon the last, propelling you toward a life of deeper fulfillment and meaningful prosperity.

Chapter 5

Overcoming Financial Blocks

Overcoming financial blocks is a matter that touches the core of our beliefs and attitudes towards money. It's not just about having more or spending less; it's about understanding the invisible forces that hold us back from realizing true abundance. These barriers are often rooted in deeply ingrained patterns and perceptions formed earlier in life, which can quietly sabotage even the most determined efforts at financial growth. Many of us carry forward these outdated ideas without realizing how they color our decisions, shaping a financial reality that feels limiting instead of expansive. Confronting these beliefs involves a journey inward to unearth and release mental blockages that keep wealth at bay. This process invites individuals to reflect on their personal history with money, considering how past influences have led to present limitations.

In this chapter, we're exploring practical solutions for identifying and dismantling these financial blocks, offering readers transformative strategies to clear away negativity and make space for prosperity. By delving into approaches such as Emotional Freedom Techniques (EFT), meditation, and affirmations, you'll discover how to tap into your inner potential and attract abundance with clarity and confidence. We will guide you through the power of mindful practices that tune your focus toward positive financial outcomes, replacing scarcity-driven thoughts with those of empowerment and belief in limitless possibilities. Plus, we'll discuss the importance of community and shared experiences, highlighting the support systems available to reinforce your journey to financial freedom. As you navigate these insights and tools, you may find yourself opening up to new ways of thinking about money—ways that align with both your spiritual and practical aspirations, setting a foundation for enduring wealth and personal growth.

TECHNIQUES FOR RELEASING RESISTANCE TO WEALTH

To overcome financial blocks, it's vital to first recognize and identify limiting beliefs around money. Many of these beliefs are ingrained from childhood experiences and messages we received about wealth. For instance, if you heard often that "money is hard to come by," this belief might linger in your subconscious, subtly influencing your financial decisions and perceptions of abundance. Reflecting on such early teachings allows you to uncover these deep-seated notions. Consider how comments or attitudes you observed as a child have shaped your current mindset. Did family members express fear of not having enough? Were there criticisms aimed at those who had wealth? These reflections can unveil the origins of mental barriers obstructing financial success.

Once these limiting beliefs are identified, it's crucial to adopt effective releasing techniques. One powerful method is EFT (Emotional Freedom Techniques), also known as tapping. This practice involves lightly tapping on specific pressure points while focusing on negative emotions or thoughts to release them. Detailed guidance is essential for effectively implementing EFT, which begins with identifying specific beliefs to be addressed. Then, while stating these beliefs aloud, tap on key meridian points like the side of the hand, eyebrows, and under the eyes. Emphasizing consistency is important here; regular practice can lead to tangible improvements in diminishing resistance to wealth. As you progress, you may find that your relationship with money becomes more fluid and less stress-inducing.

Another supportive approach is meditative practices that harness specific tools and sound frequencies designed to shift your mental state towards welcoming abundance. Engaging in meditation caters to tuning out distractions and recalibrating focus onto what is desirable financially. By incorporating sound frequencies, such as solfeggio frequencies known to enhance spiritual healing, you amplify the potential for change. Visualization techniques can further strengthen this connection, inviting prosperity into your life by vividly imagining the fulfillment of your financial goals. Picture yourself achieving financial milestones, feeling secure, and living abundantly. Regular meditation fosters a constructive mindset, gradually replacing skepticism with trust in your journey to wealth.

Affirmation strategies form another essential component of nurturing an abundant mindset. Crafting personalized affirmations tailored to your unique aspirations can affect profound internal change. The key to effective affirmations lies not only in repetition but in genuine emotional engagement. Start with statements beginning with "I am" that reflect positive qualities or achievements, like "I am attracting wealth effortlessly." Practice these daily, ideally in a calm setting where you can truly absorb the words. As you repeat these affirmations, feel the emotions they evoke—gratitude, joy, or excitement about your financial future. This process helps reprogram negative thought patterns, replacing them with empowering beliefs aligned with abundance.

Moreover, it's beneficial to maintain a journal dedicated to these practices, tracking progress, insights, and any shifts in beliefs. Writing reinforces new ideas and solidifies the commitment to change. Document circumstances where you successfully identified and challenged a limiting belief. Record moments when meditation facilitated a breakthrough in perception, or when affirmation use resulted in noticeable positivity. This documentation serves as both a tool for reflection and a motivational record of personal growth.

Engaging with community support can also bolster efforts in overcoming financial barriers. Sharing experiences and insights with like-minded individuals can provide encouragement and new perspectives. Attend workshops or online forums dedicated to financial mindfulness and holistic wealth-building approaches. These spaces offer opportunities for exchanging helpful practices and learning from others' successes and challenges. Cultivating connections within such communities fosters a sense of support and collective ambition toward financial empowerment.

The Importance of Reframing Financial Setbacks

When we talk about financial setbacks, it's easy to label them as failures and move on. But what if we saw these moments not as defeats, but as pivotal steps forward in our journey? By changing our perspective, setbacks can become vital learning experiences. Financial setbacks are often caused by patterns that create stagnation—repeated behaviors or decisions that might be subtle but significantly impact our financial growth. By identifying these patterns, we can start viewing financial setbacks as essential feedback for personal development rather than frustrating dead-ends.

Recognizing the value of setbacks is one thing, but cultivating a mindset that can thrive amidst these challenges requires effort and curiosity. Imagine approaching obstacles with the same intrigue a scientist has when conducting an experiment—no failure, just data. This shift from despair to curiosity is crucial in turning setbacks into opportunities. Consider seeking out success stories or creating networks with like-minded individuals who have faced similar situations. Communities provide emotional support and share practical advice that empowers others to rewrite their financial narratives, fostering a resilient outlook towards wealth acquisition.

Sometimes, though, we need concrete tools to help us reframe our thinking around setbacks. This is where practical reframing techniques come into play. By actively documenting lessons learned from financial hurdles, you can track your personal growth over time.

This act of reflection not only highlights progress but also builds a repository of resilience strategies and insights that prepare you for future challenges. One effective approach is to keep a journal where you record each setback alongside the silver lining it presented—this exercise reinforces the habit of seeing beyond immediate disappointment to longer-term benefits.

Turning setbacks into defining goals requires a thoughtful transformation of insights into actions. It's not enough to simply extract wisdom from past mistakes; we must use those lessons to shape clear, actionable objectives. Applying SMART (Specific, Measurable, Achievable, Relevant, Time-bound) goals is an excellent way to tie past experiences with a structured plan for the future. For example, if a financial misstep taught you the importance of budgeting, a SMART goal could involve setting monthly spending limits with corresponding savings targets. This method ensures that each lesson is quickly converted into a step toward greater financial abundance.

To integrate guidelines effectively, consider strategies that foster a growth mindset. Start by consciously replacing critical self-talk with questions that spark curiosity: "What did this teach me?", "How can I do better next time?" Having a supportive network of peers or mentors can amplify this mindset shift. Engage in conversations with people who inspire and challenge you to see potential rather than pitfalls in every financial twist. Encourage sharing of personal triumphs and setbacks within these groups; collective storytelling can be a powerful motivator, demonstrating that persistence pays off more than perfection.

Practical reframing involves tools that clarify lessons from setbacks while preparing for future resilience. Here, guidelines can make a difference. Regularly set aside time to reflect on both current victories and past challenges, noting how they interconnect. Documentation becomes your ally; maintaining a detailed ledger of experiences helps identify recurring themes and offers proof of progress during discouraging times. Planning actionable responses before you face adversity can also cushion the blow when setbacks occur, ensuring you're equipped to handle them gracefully.

Using setbacks to define goals is another area where specific guidelines can bolster your efforts. Employing the SMART framework will guide your trajectory from insight to achievement efficiently. Begin by clearly articulating each objective based on past financial learnings. Ensure your goals are measurable so progress can be tracked, making the path to abundance tangible and motivating. Adjust these goals as needed, remaining flexible yet focused on the overarching aim of financial empowerment and freedom.

THOUGHTS

In this chapter, we've explored how deeply ingrained beliefs can block our path to financial success and how uncovering these can be empowering. Often, these limiting beliefs have roots in childhood, influencing how we perceive wealth without us even realizing it. By using techniques like EFT tapping and meditation, we begin to dismantle these mental barriers, making room for a healthier relationship with money. These practices, along with journaling and community support, provide practical steps to help transform your mindset towards abundance. They encourage you to recognize and challenge the subconscious narratives that may have held you back, helping to pave a smoother road to achieving your financial goals.

As you move forward, remember that adopting new habits and attitudes about wealth requires patience and persistence. By incorporating affirmations and cultivating a growth-oriented mindset, you're setting a strong foundation for lasting change. This shift is not just about gaining wealth but also about embracing a holistic approach to prosperity that aligns with your personal and spiritual aspirations. Through consistent application of these strategies—be it reframing setbacks or setting actionable goals—you empower yourself to navigate financial challenges with resilience and confidence. Your journey toward financial empowerment is an ongoing process, filled with learning opportunities, that will enrich every aspect of your life.

Chapter 6

Reprogramming the Subconscious Mind

Reprogramming the subconscious mind is about unlocking hidden potential within ourselves to reshape our financial realities. It's an empowering journey that encourages us to delve deeper into our psyche and challenge long-held beliefs about money. We often underestimate how much our ingrained thoughts influence our financial decisions. However, when we learn to recognize these patterns, we open the door to change. Through deliberate practices aimed at rewiring our mental frameworks, we can transform our mindset toward one of wealth and abundance. This transformation not only propels us toward achieving our financial desires but also enhances the confidence required to pursue them.

In this chapter, a variety of strategies will be explored to help you reprogram your subconscious for financial success. You'll discover engaging visualization techniques that assist in aligning your mental focus with prosperity, creating tangible goals, and maintaining motivation. Vision boards, guided imagery, and future self-visualization will be covered, offering practical tools to manifest a wealth-oriented mindset. Additionally, the chapter delves into using meditative visualization to harmonize with the frequency of abundance, providing pathways to let go of limiting beliefs. These practices are designed to be accessible and easy to integrate into your daily routine, making the process both practical and transformative. Whether you are new to these concepts or looking to deepen your understanding, this chapter offers insights and methods to support your journey towards financial empowerment.

Visualization Techniques for Wealth Mindset

In the exploration of reprogramming our subconscious minds, visualization stands as a pivotal practice that bridges our current reality with the wealth and abundance we aspire to attain. Using visualization techniques effectively can transform our financial mindset and align our thoughts with prosperity.

Vision boards offer a powerful way to engage our emotions in this journey. By creating collages of images and affirmations that symbolize our wealth goals, we establish tangible reminders of the abundance we seek. The process of selecting images that resonate with our aspirations helps anchor these desires deep within our subconscious. For example, envisioning a dream home or a thriving business on your vision board facilitates a strong emotional connection. This connection acts as a motivator, encouraging continuous reflection on these objectives and gradually aligning our daily actions toward achieving them.

For those interested in crafting these impactful tools, consider using a mix of images that not only represent large-scale financial goals but also smaller, easily attainable ones. Begin by gathering materials such as magazines, photographs, and printed words that resonate with your idea of abundance. Arrange these items on a board where you can see them regularly, allowing their energy to become part of your daily environment.

Guided imagery offers another layer of transformation by involving the mind in vividly picturing scenarios of abundance. Through structured sessions, individuals can explore imaginative scenes where they have reached their desired state of wealth. This immersive experience rewires self-perception and beliefs about money, fostering confidence in one's ability to attract prosperity. For instance, imagine yourself walking into a luxurious office or receiving recognition for your financial achievements; these visions can break down internal barriers and reshape how you view your potential.

To practice guided imagery effectively, find a quiet space, free from interruptions. Close your eyes and visualize specific situations where you experience financial success. Engage all your senses during this practice — feel the textures, hear the sounds, and notice the finer details. Consistency is key, so integrate this exercise into your routine to continually reinforce these positive impressions.

Furthermore, future self-visualization serves as a tool to clarify actionable steps towards living in financial abundance. By imagining a day in the life of your future self who has already achieved financial success, you can identify the habits, decisions, and strategies that led you there. This form of visualization not only strengthens motivation but also provides a clearer roadmap for making effective choices in the present. Consider envisioning yourself engaging in activities that reflect your wealth goals, such as investing wisely or contributing to meaningful causes. These images serve as mental rehearsals, conditioning your mind to adopt the attitudes and behaviors necessary for realizing these dreams.

To delve into future self-visualization, allocate time daily to reflect on these scenarios. Ask yourself questions like: What kind of lifestyle does my future self enjoy? What steps did I take to get here? By consistently envisioning these answers, you'll start naturally gravitating towards actions that manifest your desired outcomes.

Meditative visualization further harmonizes individuals with the frequency of abundance through focused practice. This technique involves reaching a meditative state where one's mental energy aligns with the vibrations of prosperity. By centering your thoughts on abundant feelings and experiences during meditation, you foster a sense of peace and assurance in your ability to achieve financial growth. This method allows practitioners to let go of limiting beliefs and embrace an abundant mindset with openness and acceptance.

When practicing meditative visualization, find a comfortable position and focus on your breath. Once relaxed, bring to mind images of wealth and prosperity. Let these pictures fill your consciousness without judgment or doubt. Feel the positive emotions associated with these visions and maintain this state for a few minutes each day. Over time, this will help solidify your connection to the abundant universe around you.

Harnessing Affirmations for Financial Prosperity

Affirmations are powerful tools that can profoundly transform our subconscious beliefs and help establish a mindset oriented toward abundance. By altering the foundational thoughts within us, affirmations pave the way for achieving financial prosperity.

To begin with, crafting personalized affirmations is crucial. The personalization aspect ensures an emotional resonance that standard or generic affirmations might miss. The language you choose should deeply resonate with your core values and unique ambitions. For instance, instead of using general phrases like "I am wealthy," you might say, "I attract abundant opportunities that align with my purpose." This specificity not only makes the affirmation more relatable but also strengthens its power by building a deeper connection between your conscious desires and subconscious beliefs.

Moreover, crafting these tailored affirmations does more than just create emotional connections—it acts as a guiding light on manifestation pathways. When you frame affirmations in a way that aligns with your personal goals, they start to guide your actions and decisions subconsciously, influencing the paths you take toward wealth creation. For example, if you're aiming for entrepreneurial success, framing affirmations around innovation and growth can subtly steer your mind toward spotting business opportunities.

The magic of affirmations doesn't end at their creation; repetition plays a vital role in integrating these positive statements into the subconscious mind. Repetition helps in overwriting negative, limiting beliefs that may have been ingrained over years. By frequently repeating affirmations, whether silently, out loud, or even through written form, you gradually start replacing old thought patterns with new ones that support your goals. It is similar to learning a new skill—the more you practice, the better you become at it. To maximize their effectiveness, consider setting a specific time each day dedicated to reciting your affirmations, such as during your morning routine or before bedtime.

Furthermore, while repetition is important, it's the emotional resonance felt during affirmation practice that significantly accelerates alignment with desired financial outcomes. Engaging emotions while saying affirmations amplifies their effect on the subconscious mind. When you truly feel the words you're speaking—when you visualize them, embody them, and experience the joy they bring—you heighten their impact. Imagine the satisfaction of a financial goal attained; feel the excitement, relief, and gratitude as though it's happening now. Such potent emotional engagement acts as a catalyst, propelling you toward manifesting those outcomes in real life.

Adding another dimension to this practice is sharing affirmations within supportive communities. Involving others helps bolster your commitment and offers a sense of accountability. When you join groups or forums focused on affirmations and personal growth, you tap into collective energy and motivation. Engaging with like-minded individuals provides encouragement and reinforces the belief that change is possible. For example, participating in online communities where members regularly share successes achieved through affirmations can strengthen your resolve to stay committed to the process. Encouragement from peers experiencing similar journeys can propel you further along your path.

Even outside formal communities, simply sharing affirmations with trusted friends or family can be beneficial. When you voice your affirmations to others, it adds a layer of validation to your intentions and fosters mutual support. Sharing also opens dialogues about shared goals and insights, enhancing personal growth and resilience against setbacks.

Concluding Thoughts

In this chapter, we've delved into the powerful world of subconscious programming to reshape your financial mindset. Through visualization techniques like vision boards and guided imagery, you've discovered how these mental exercises can create a bridge between your current reality and future financial goals. By immersing yourself in vivid images of wealth and success, you are actively setting the stage for real transformation. The consistent practice of these techniques empowers you to break free from limiting beliefs and align your thoughts and actions with prosperity. Emotional engagement is key here, allowing you to feel and embody the abundance you seek, ultimately manifesting it in your life.

Additionally, we've explored the role of affirmations in transforming your subconscious thoughts and guiding your journey toward financial abundance. Crafting personalized affirmations that resonate deeply with your aspirations ensures they serve as effective tools for change. Repetition and emotional resonance during affirmation practice help rewire your thought patterns, replacing negative beliefs with empowering ones. Sharing your affirmations within supportive communities adds an extra layer of accountability and inspiration. Together, these strategies provide a holistic approach to reprogramming your mind for wealth, offering actionable steps to help you embrace a financially abundant future with confidence and optimism.

Chapter 7

Maintaining Alignment with the Wealth Frequency

Aligning your life with the wealth frequency is all about tuning your mindset and daily habits towards prosperity. It's a journey that blends personal growth with practical strategies, demanding attention to both the tangible and intangible aspects of wealth. By focusing on this alignment, you set the stage for not just acquiring abundance but sustaining it over time. The concept goes beyond mere financial gain; it encompasses developing an enriched life where joy, fulfillment, and freedom are abundant. This chapter delves into the core principles behind maintaining this alignment, offering insights into how consistent practices can nurture both your spirit and bank account.

In this chapter, you'll explore long-term strategies designed to keep your energy attuned to abundance. You'll learn about establishing personalized wealth rituals that include techniques like gratitude practices and visualization exercises to sustain an open channel to prosperity. There's a focus on cultivating an abundant mindset by replacing limiting beliefs with empowering affirmations, along with creating an environment conducive to attracting wealth through organization and positive influences. The chapter also covers the importance of self-monitoring energy levels and making necessary adjustments, using tools like journaling and energy check-ins to ensure you remain on track. Whether it's engaging in community support or reassessing your money beliefs, each technique is carefully crafted to help you harness the wealth frequency fully. Through these approaches, you'll be equipped to transform your relationship with money, making abundance a permanent part of your existence.

Long-term Strategies to Stay Connected to Abundance

To achieve a harmonious alignment with prosperity over the long term, it is critical to develop sustainable practices and habits. Your energy consistently attuned to abundance can lead to lasting financial empowerment and fulfillment. One powerful approach to maintaining this connection is by establishing daily wealth rituals tailored to your unique needs. These rituals might include gratitude exercises, which help you recognize and appreciate the wealth already present in your life. By starting each day with a focus on gratitude, you open yourself up to receiving more blessings and wealth. Energy cleansing practices, such as meditation or mindful breathing, can also be integrated into these rituals to clear any blocks and invite freshness and renewal into your financial sphere.

Incorporating these practices requires consistency and personalization. Simply put, the key is to design a routine that resonates deeply with you and encourages a regular engagement with wealth energy. For instance, setting aside a quiet time each morning to journal about financial aspirations or visualize achieving financial milestones can significantly enhance your focus and reinforce your commitment to prosperity. Tailoring these practices ensures they become an intrinsic part of your daily life, acting as a continuous reminder of your journey toward abundance.

Cultivating an abundant mindset forms another vital pillar in aligning with wealth frequency. This involves consciously replacing scarcity-driven thoughts with positive affirmations. For example, instead of dwelling on what you lack, affirm statements like "I am worthy of wealth and abundance" to gradually transform your thinking patterns. Such affirmations work by reprogramming your subconscious mind, steering it away from fear-based scarcity and towards a natural state of prosperity.

Surrounding yourself with positive influences can further strengthen this mindset shift. Engage with communities, read literature, or listen to content that uplifts and encourages an abundant way of thinking. When surrounded by people who advocate for growth and resilience, you start to mirror their optimism, infusing your own life with similar energy. This nurturing of an abundant mindset can alter neural pathways, fostering a mental environment where success and prosperity thrive naturally.

Setting clear, measurable, and emotionally resonant financial intentions is crucial for aligning oneself with wealth energy. The process of intention setting goes beyond mere wishful thinking; it involves a deliberate declaration of your financial goals alongside a plan of action. Regularly revisiting these intentions ensures accountability and keeps your motivation alive.

Visualization techniques are particularly effective in this context. Picture yourself living out your financial dreams, using all your senses to make the experience vivid and compelling. Imagine feeling the sensation of victory, seeing the results, hearing the sounds associated with achievement. This immersive practice reinforces your commitment and aligns your emotional and cognitive faculties with your financial objectives, making them feel achievable and within reach.

Finally, creating a prosperity environment can significantly enhance your alignment with abundance. Begin by decluttering and organizing your living and working spaces. An organized environment reduces distractions and creates a flow of energy conducive to productivity and attraction of wealth. Incorporate symbols of wealth and abundance, be it through art, tokens, or even colors associated with prosperity like green and gold. These visual cues serve as constant reminders of your goals and the lifestyle you aspire to live.

Additionally, consider integrating elements of nature into your space, such as plants, which are often associated with growth and vitality. The presence of these elements can amplify the energetic atmosphere, making it more attuned to the flow of abundance. Remember that your physical space reflects your internal state, so maintaining a tidy, aesthetically pleasing environment not only nurtures creativity but also invites prosperity into your life.

While implementing these strategies may seem overwhelming initially, remember that the path to sustained wealth frequency is a personal and evolving journey. Start small, perhaps by adopting one or two practices, and gradually expand your repertoire as you become more comfortable and aligned with these routines. Over time, these practices will become second nature, effortlessly supporting your ongoing connection to abundance.

Monitoring Personal Energy Levels and Making Adjustments

In the pursuit of maintaining alignment with the wealth frequency, it's crucial to recognize and manage fluctuations in our personal energy relating to financial well-being. This process begins with practicing self-awareness, an essential component for anyone looking to identify patterns that might be influencing their financial path. Keeping a journal dedicated to your financial feelings can serve as a powerful tool for this purpose. By regularly documenting your thoughts and emotions regarding money, you can start to see recurring themes or obstacles that may be affecting how you interact with wealth.

For instance, you might notice a pattern where every time an unexpected expense arises, it triggers anxiety or fear. By recognizing this response, you can take steps to address these feelings, ultimately leading to more informed decisions on your journey toward financial prosperity. Journaling is not just about capturing negative experiences; it also provides a space to celebrate financial successes, reinforcing positive behavior and offering insights into what strategies are working for you.

Another important practice is conducting regular energy check-ins throughout the day. These check-ins act as moments of pause where you assess your current state and make adjustments if needed. Consider setting aside short intervals, perhaps at the start and end of each day, to reflect on your energy levels and how they relate to your financial goals. Are you feeling distracted or overwhelmed? Are there specific stresses or habits that are pulling your focus away from achieving those aspirations?

These energy check-ins can also help clear mental clutter, making room for a clearer focus on what truly matters financially. They enable resilience by offering a chance to recalibrate and refocus, ensuring you're consistently moving towards your objectives and maintaining a steady course toward prosperity.

To further support your alignment with the wealth frequency, utilizing energy tools and techniques can significantly enhance your ability to readjust your energetic vibrations. Sound healing, meditation, and Emotional Freedom Techniques (EFT) tapping are just a few methods that can aid in this realignment. These practices can help shift your mindset from scarcity to abundance, providing a more solid foundation for attracting wealth.

Sound healing, for example, uses specific frequencies to bring balance to your body's energy centers, promoting relaxation and clarity. Meditation offers a space for introspection and transformation by quieting the mind and allowing deeper insights and solutions related to financial challenges to arise. Meanwhile, EFT tapping combines elements of acupressure and cognitive therapies to reduce stress and release emotional blockages, empowering you to move forward with a stronger, more positive stance towards wealth.

While tools and techniques are vital, reassessing and challenging limiting beliefs around money must not be overlooked. Our beliefs heavily influence our reality, particularly in terms of financial well-being. By becoming aware of any negative or restrictive beliefs you hold about money, you can begin replacing them with empowering alternatives. For instance, if you've always believed that being wealthy means being greedy, you could transform this belief by acknowledging that financial abundance allows for greater generosity and improved quality of life.

Engaging with supportive communities can greatly assist in this endeavor. Surrounding yourself with like-minded individuals who share similar financial values and goals creates an environment where dynamic energy flow thrives, opening new doors and opportunities. Such communities offer encouragement, shared wisdom, and accountability, all of which bolster your energy alignment with wealth. By participating in groups, whether in person or online, that focus on positive financial growth, you tap into a collective mindset that nurtures progress and possibility.

THOUGHTS

In this chapter, we've delved into the vital process of aligning your energy with prosperity. By integrating personalized and consistent rituals, you can keep your focus on gratitude and abundance as a natural part of your everyday life. The key lies in nurturing an abundant mindset, enriched by positive affirmations and supportive communities that encourage growth and optimism. These strategies help reframe your thoughts, shifting them away from scarcity and guiding you toward a prosperous outlook. By setting clear financial intentions and using visualization techniques, you create a vivid picture of your goals, making them feel both achievable and within reach.

Moving forward, it's essential to monitor your personal energy levels and make necessary adjustments to stay in tune with wealth frequency. Self-awareness plays a crucial role here; it allows you to identify patterns affecting your financial well-being and address them proactively. Regular journaling and energy check-ins act as valuable tools in maintaining focus and resilience. Additionally, exploring energy tools like sound healing and meditation can support your journey, helping you overcome limiting beliefs and stay aligned with abundance. Remember, your path to financial empowerment and alignment with prosperity is an evolving one, so embrace each step with openness and readiness for growth.

Chapter 8

Integrating Spiritual Wisdom with Practical Finance

Blending spiritual wisdom with practical finance is a dynamic approach to achieving true financial abundance. This chapter invites you on a journey that aligns your inner beliefs with the realities of managing wealth in the modern world. It's an exploration of how deeply interconnected our spiritual insights and financial strategies can be, suggesting that a harmonious relationship between the two can lead to profound results. By integrating these seemingly distinct aspects, you can open pathways to not just financial success, but also personal fulfillment. The essence lies in recognizing that wealth is not just about material gain but also about nurturing an abundance mindset rooted in spiritual alignment.

In this chapter, you'll delve into transformative ideas like balancing metaphysical principles with real-world financial practices. Concepts such as the Law of Attraction will be demystified, showing how focusing on positive energy can manifest tangible financial outcomes. You'll discover the power of intentional budgeting aligned with your core values, providing a framework for spending that enhances both peace of mind and prosperity. Practical tools like meditation and vision boards are introduced, offering creative ways to visualize and achieve your financial goals while staying grounded in mindfulness. Additionally, learn about the significance of gratitude and acts of service in amplifying abundance, exploring how generosity and spiritual grounding can bring a flow of wealth into your life. Whether you're a seasoned practitioner of spiritual methods or new to the idea, this chapter offers insightful strategies for integrating spiritual teachings with actionable financial techniques to enhance your journey toward comprehensive wealth alignment.

BALANCING METAPHYSICAL PRINCIPLES WITH REAL-WORLD FINANCE

Integrating spiritual principles with financial strategies is a powerful approach to managing wealth effectively and holistically. One of the core concepts in this integration is understanding the flow of abundance. Financial abundance is often perceived as an external achievement, yet it originates from within. To truly comprehend this, one must embrace the notion that abundance is a natural state, attainable through spiritual insights and practices.

Spiritual teachings often highlight the idea that abundance flows when we are aligned with our true purpose and values. By tapping into this inner wisdom, you can recognize opportunities that resonate with your personal journey and bring prosperity. For example, consider how ancient philosophies such as Taoism emphasize living in harmony with the universe. This harmony extends to finances, where aligning your actions with your spiritual beliefs naturally cultivates abundance.

Next, applying the Law of Attraction to finances involves focusing on positive outcomes to manifest tangible results. The Law of Attraction suggests that what we focus on expands. In financial terms, directing your thoughts toward abundance rather than scarcity plays a crucial role in manifesting wealth. Picture someone who constantly worries about not having enough money; this mindset can perpetuate a cycle of lack. Conversely, maintaining a mindset rich with gratitude and optimism attracts prosperous situations and resources.

To practice this, regularly visualize your financial goals and affirm them positively. Instead of dwelling on debts, imagine being debt-free and financially secure. Create a routine where each day starts with recounting three things you're grateful for financially – perhaps a stable job, unexpected gains, or simple pleasures like a cup of coffee. Cultivating this positivity shifts your energy towards a more abundant life.

Guidelines for using the Law of Attraction include setting clear intentions, visualizing desired outcomes vividly, and taking inspired actions aligned with these intentions. By combining these elements, you create a magnetic field that draws your financial aspirations closer to reality. Moreover, it's essential to stay open to opportunities that may arise unexpectedly, as they could lead to significant financial improvements.

In addition to mental alignment, integrating meditation into money management enhances clarity and decision-making processes. Meditation fosters mindfulness, reducing stress and fostering a calm mind, which is crucial when making financial choices. When you're grounded and centered, you can evaluate options more objectively, ensuring decisions align with both practical needs and spiritual values.

Consider a daily meditation practice focusing on financial peace and clarity. Sit quietly for ten minutes each day, breathing deeply, and visualize your financial goals unfolding effortlessly. Over time, this routine strengthens your ability to remain calm under pressure, improving your reactions to financial challenges. This mindful approach aids in reducing impulsive spending and encourages thoughtful investments.

Another valuable tool is creating a vision board for financial goals. Vision boards serve as a creative outlet to manifest and visualize your desired financial life. By collecting images and words representing your financial objectives, you reinforce your belief in their attainment. This visual representation keeps your goals at the forefront of your consciousness and serves as a daily reminder of what you're working towards.

To construct an effective vision board, take some time to reflect on your financial dreams. What does financial freedom look like to you? Gather images from magazines, online sources, or even draw your own representations of these goals. Arrange them on a board and place it somewhere you'll see it often. Regularly update it as your goals evolve or reach fruition. Every glance at the board reinforces your commitment and energizes your pursuit of these ambitions.

While crafting your vision board, engage your senses. Imagine the emotions tied to achieving these goals—excitement, relief, joy—and let those feelings anchor your intentions. By infusing emotion into this exercise, you amplify its power, turning it into a dynamic part of your financial journey.

CREATING A HOLISTIC FINANCIAL PLAN USING SPIRITUAL TOOLS

In the realm of blending spiritual wisdom with practical finance, starting with a clear understanding of one's personal values and financial goals is the cornerstone for creating an integrated plan. It's essential to recognize how deeply our spiritual beliefs can shape the way we approach money management. Aligning financial objectives with personal missions can lead to more meaningful wealth creation. For instance, consider someone whose value system prioritizes environmental sustainability. Their financial goals might include investing in green technologies or supporting companies that uphold eco-friendly practices. This alignment creates not just monetary benefits but also deep satisfaction and fulfillment as every financial decision resonates with their core values.

As you embark on defining your financial journey, reflect on what truly matters to you. Are there particular causes or lifestyles you are passionate about? By clarifying these priorities, you help ensure that your financial plan is a true reflection of who you are. This reflective practice lays the foundation for a deliberate approach to money, one that fosters genuine happiness rather than temporary satisfaction.

Once your values and goals are clearly defined, the next step is budgeting with intention. Intentional budgeting is about designing a budget that honors your spiritual beliefs and values, allowing for conscious spending that brings peace of mind. Unlike traditional budgeting approaches that might focus solely on dollars and cents, intentional budgeting considers the impact of each spending choice on your emotional and spiritual state. It encourages spending in ways that support both your basic needs and your higher aspirations.

To effectively create an intentional budget, start by reviewing your current spending habits. Identify areas where expenditures do not align with your values, and make adjustments accordingly. A simple guideline could be allocating funds toward experiences and items that nourish the soul, such as mindfulness classes or donations to charitable organizations. Tracking these expenses helps maintain balance, ensuring that each dollar spent contributes positively to both your material and spiritual well-being.

Incorporating affirmations into your financial planning can further cement success by reinforcing positive behaviors and dispelling limiting beliefs. Affirmations are powerful statements that, when repeated regularly, reshape thought patterns and foster a mindset geared towards abundance. Many people find that affirmations such as "I am open to receiving limitless prosperity" or "My wealth grows as I enrich others" provide daily motivation and reinforce a positive outlook.

To maximize the effectiveness of affirmations, speak them aloud each morning or evening as part of a ritualistic practice. Visualize the outcomes as if they have already occurred, thereby anchoring these possibilities in your reality. This consistent practice builds confidence and gradually transforms doubts into conviction, aligning your mental state with your financial aspirations.

Engaging in acts of service and gratitude serves as another dynamic method of integrating spirituality with finance. Generosity, whether through philanthropy or everyday kindness, amplifies your wealth frequency by inviting the flow of abundance into your life. History and wisdom traditions across cultures teach us that giving from a place of authenticity and love returns tenfold, enhancing both material and spiritual prosperity.

Consider volunteering your time or sharing resources with those in need. These actions not only make a tangible difference in others' lives but also cultivate inner richness. Practicing gratitude for the blessings already present in your life, regardless of your current financial situation, shifts focus from scarcity to abundance. This shift invites more opportunities and growth, affirming the belief that there is always enough to share.

Concluding Thoughts

Throughout this chapter, we've delved into the enriching blend of spiritual insights and practical financial techniques to bring about a holistic alignment of one's wealth journey. Recognizing abundance as an inherent potential, we explored how embracing our spiritual beliefs can create a harmonious financial reality. Whether through aligning with the universe like ancient philosophies suggest or practicing the Law of Attraction, these insights invite us to shift our mindset from scarcity to gratitude, ultimately fostering prosperity. By integrating meditation and visualization exercises, we learned to enhance clarity in decision-making, allowing us to make thoughtful choices that resonate with both our spiritual values and financial goals.

As we wrap up, consider how adopting these practices can transform your financial landscape into one that truly reflects who you are. Intentional budgeting emerges as a key tool, ensuring your spending aligns with what you value most deeply. By setting clear intentions and engaging in daily affirmations, you strengthen the foundation for achieving your aspirations. Additionally, acts of service and gratitude further enrich your life, opening channels for abundance and reminding us that generosity nurtures wealth. Embracing these principles offers a path to not only financial success but also personal fulfillment, aligning your outer financial world with your inner beliefs.

Chapter 9

The Gateway to Wealth Consciousness

Entering the Higher Field of Wealth Consciousness

What if your path to wealth was never about chasing money—but accessing a state of consciousness that naturally magnetizes it? In this chapter, we step into the extraordinary intersection where science, mysticism, and philosophy unite—revealing a powerful, and long-hidden, secret: consciousness is not just the observer of wealth, it is the creator of it.

The CIA's once-classified *Gateway Process* provides compelling insight into how altered states of consciousness can allow individuals to transcend limitations of time, space, and even financial scarcity. When aligned with the teachings of visionary minds like Jacobo Grinberg, Neville Goddard, and Jiddu Krishnamurti, a transformative truth emerges: your ability to manifest wealth lies not in what you do, but in how you perceive, feel, and vibrate.

The Gateway Process and the Frequency of Wealth

In the early 1980s, the U.S. Central Intelligence Agency sponsored an exploration into the very frontier of human potential—what became known as *The Gateway Process*.

Based on research by the Monroe Institute, this classified program focused on using sound frequencies (Hemi-Sync) to help subjects achieve altered states of consciousness. The goal? Remote viewing, reality manipulation, and non-local perception—concepts once reserved for mystics and metaphysicians.

But buried within those intentions was a deeper discovery: when the mind enters deeply coherent, hemispherically synchronized brain states, it becomes an active *participant* in shaping reality—not a passive observer. The same theta and delta frequencies triggered during Gateway sessions mirror the states we've discussed throughout this book—the exact frequencies where financial intentions crystallize and manifest.

The same vibrational laws of attraction, visualization, and emotional coherence we've studied are *amplified* in the Gateway process. It's a powerful validation: science has not only caught up to spiritual truths—it has confirmed them.

JACOBO GRINBERG AND THE CONSCIOUSNESS FIELD OF WEALTH

The late Mexican neuroscientist Jacobo Grinberg proposed a remarkable idea through his *Syntergy Theory*: that all of reality is shaped by a unified field of consciousness—a matrix that responds directly to human perception and emotion.

Grinberg's studies with indigenous shamans revealed that consciousness could bend time, space, and matter. Shamans would influence weather, retrieve information from distant locations, and affect health outcomes—all through *focused consciousness*. Sound familiar?

What the CIA studied in controlled labs—Grinberg saw in the field.

Now, imagine that same universal field attuned to the frequency of abundance. If money is energy, and energy responds to coherent consciousness, then the path to wealth isn't about labor—it's about *resonance*.

When you visualize wealth, align your emotion with gratitude, and embody abundance energetically, you imprint the Syntergy Field—just as the Gateway participants influenced reality through brain synchronization.

Practical Insight:
When practicing your daily meditation or affirmations, imagine your thoughts *bending* the field. Feel the ripple expanding outwards—adjusting circumstances, magnetizing wealth, and creating synchronicities. Your wealth field is not imagined—it is real, and it responds.

NEVILLE GODDARD AND THE POWER OF IMAGINAL WEALTH

If Grinberg offered the science, Neville Goddard gave us the technique.

Goddard's central teaching was bold and clear: *"Assume the feeling of the wish fulfilled."* To him, imagination wasn't daydreaming—it was creation. When you imagine yourself already wealthy, already grateful, already abundant—you cause reality to conform to that state.

Gateway training used theta-state induction to enter a liminal zone between sleep and wakefulness—the exact same brainwave Goddard encouraged during his manifestation exercises. The body is relaxed. The conscious mind quiet. The subconscious open.

This is the sacred gateway—where intention becomes instruction.

In your wealth practice, visualize with detail: the sights, sounds, and sensations of your prosperous life. Don't hope for it. Feel it. Know it. Goddard believed if you stayed in that imaginal state consistently, the outer world must reflect it. Gateway scientists found the same: intention fused with coherent brainwaves created observable outcomes.

JIDDU KRISHNAMURTI AND THE OBSERVER'S LIBERATION FROM LACK

Enter the philosopher. Jiddu Krishnamurti did not teach about money—but he taught about freedom, and no financial transformation can occur without freeing the mind.

Krishnamurti said, *"The observer is the observed."* In wealth terms: the way you *see* your financial life is what *creates* your financial life. If you observe it with fear, lack, or guilt—you reinforce those vibrations. If you observe it with clarity, detachment, and openness—you free yourself from inherited patterns.

The Gateway Process started with a preparatory phase called *Focus 10*—where participants detached from the body and thoughts to become pure awareness.

Krishnamurti taught the same: a clean break from psychological conditioning reveals inner truth.

Practical Application:

Begin noticing your financial thoughts—not judging, but *observing*. "I'm always broke," "Money never lasts," "I can't afford that." These are subconscious programs. By becoming aware without resistance, you dissolve them. You regain authorship. And you return to the abundant self who knows: money flows to clarity.

The Unification—Gateway, Grinberg, Goddard, Krishnamurti

Though they come from different backgrounds—CIA labs, indigenous fields, mystical teachings, philosophical inquiry—Grinberg, Goddard, and Krishnamurti speak a common truth, now echoed in the Gateway Process:

> Consciousness is the master frequency. Alter it, and reality obeys.

- Grinberg gave us a scientific model for how consciousness shapes the wealth field.
- Goddard gave us a practical method to impress the subconscious and manifest prosperity.
- Krishnamurti gave us the philosophical lens to free ourselves from the illusion of scarcity.
- The Gateway Process offers a technological pathway to reach the necessary mental states.

Together, they form a complete wealth alignment system.

Closing Reflection: Your Inner Gateway Has Always Been There

You do not need CIA clearance to access your gateway. You need only commitment to consciousness.

Today, you can use binaural beats, theta meditations, and intention-setting to enter the same altered states once explored in secret labs. You can visualize as Goddard taught, free your mind as Krishnamurti guided, and impress the energetic field as Grinberg proved.

Wealth is not out there—it is activated in here.

As we enter the final chapter, you will learn how to assemble these tools into a daily practice, creating your own *wealth gateway*. What lies ahead is not just a method—but mastery.

Chapter 10

Mastering Your Personal Wealth Gateway

From Understanding to Embodiment

You've come far. You now understand that wealth is not only energy—it's consciousness in action. You've seen how frequency, intention, and the subconscious mind can be tuned like a musical instrument. And in Chapter 9, you glimpsed the deeper truth: that altered states of consciousness—once reserved for secret government projects and ancient mystics—are accessible to you right now.

Now, it's time to master this.

In this final chapter, you'll be guided through a practical and transformative system—a ritualized method that blends *The Gateway Process, Jacobo Grinberg's consciousness field, Neville Goddard's imaginal power,* and *Krishnamurti's pure awareness*. This isn't theory anymore. This is a daily gateway—a path to consistently aligning with the frequency of abundance.

Building Your Wealth Gateway Toolkit

To master wealth consciousness, you must train your internal environment the same way a musician trains their ears or an athlete trains their muscles. This begins by building your own personal Wealth Gateway Toolkit—

a daily ritual that activates your mind, aligns your frequency, and commands your reality.

<u>Key Tools:</u>

1. Binaural Beats (Hemi-Sync Technology):
   Choose audio tracks that include 528 Hz or theta wave (4–8 Hz) frequencies. These sounds help you enter deep, creative brain states. Use headphones for best effect.

2. Guided Meditation or Deep Silence:
   Use a meditation timer (or app) and set aside 15–20 minutes each morning. Sit comfortably, spine tall. Focus first on your breath, then allow your awareness to float toward your intention.

3. Imaginal Visualization (Goddard Method):
   Visualize one financial goal—in vivid detail. See yourself already living that outcome. Inhabit it emotionally. If it's business success, see the bank transfer, feel the handshake, hear your voice expressing gratitude.

4. Affirmation Embodiment:
   Choose 1–3 wealth affirmations and speak them with presence after your meditation. Example
   - *"I am the frequency of abundance."*
   - *"My consciousness shapes a prosperous reality."*
   - *"Wealth flows to me because I am tuned to receive it."*

6. Self-Inquiry Journal (Krishnamurti Method):
   Each evening, write 2–3 lines answering this prompt:

   "What did I believe about money today—and did that belief serve my abundance?"

Awareness breaks the illusion. Repetition builds a new reality.

CLEARING SUBCONSCIOUS RESISTANCE AND LIMITING BELIEFS

Before you can fill your reality with abundance, you must *clear the vessel.* Hidden within your subconscious are patterns inherited from culture, parents, religion, and past financial experiences.

These are often not logical—they are *emotional imprints.* They hide in statements like:

- "I'm just not good with money."
- "Wealth is for other people."
- "Money causes stress."

These thoughts vibrate below the frequency of wealth. Your goal is not to fight them—but to bring them to the light. *Awareness heals.*

Technique: The Mirror & Journal Method

1. Sit in front of a mirror. Breathe deeply. Say aloud:
   "Money and I are in a harmonious relationship."
2. Notice any tension, disbelief, or emotional reaction.
3. Immediately journal:
   - What did I feel in my body?
   - What memory or belief surfaced?
   - What new belief would serve me better?

Repeat this practice daily for 7–14 days.

Energy Expansion Practice (Gateway Field Exercise):

- Sit in meditation with 528 Hz audio.
- Visualize your consciousness as light expanding beyond your body.
- Imagine your energy stretching into your future—into scenes of financial ease.
- Feel gratitude ripple outward, imprinting the field.

This is *frequency imprinting*. You are not just visualizing wealth—you are instructing the universe how to respond to you.

Advanced Reality Creation—A Wealth Gateway Ritual

Now that your field is clear and activated, you're ready to use the Wealth Gateway Ritual—a full-spectrum daily practice blending all key modalities.

The Ritual (20–30 Minutes Daily):

1. Brainwave Tuning (3 minutes):
    - Use theta or 528 Hz binaural beats.
    - Breathe deeply. Relax each body part. Let go.
3. State Induction (5–7 minutes):
    - Silently affirm: *"I am safe. I am open. I am the creator."*
    - Visualize yourself stepping into your future financial self—walking through a portal or 'gateway'.

5. Imaginal Scene Construction (10–12 minutes):
   - Create a single vivid scene of a financial goal fulfilled (e.g., signing a client, receiving payment, celebrating with family).
   - Immerse all senses: sound, sight, scent, emotion.
   - Stay in that state until it feels realer than your current one.
7. Integration & Gratitude (3–5 minutes):
   - Speak your affirmations aloud with certainty.
   - Close your ritual with gratitude for what already *is* and what *is becoming*.

Repeat daily for 21 days. The brain and field respond to repetition and coherence.

Real-Life Examples & Scientific Support

You're not alone on this journey. Across the world, people have applied Gateway-style practices with profound financial transformations. Here are just a few examples:

Case Study 1: The Freelancer's Breakthrough

Ella, a freelance designer in Canada, began practicing theta meditation combined with vivid daily scenes of abundance. In less than 30 days, she landed two long-term contracts worth more than triple her usual rate. She didn't "hustle" harder—she resonated higher.

Case Study 2: Rewriting Generational Money Beliefs

Carlos grew up in poverty and inherited the belief that "money is a burden." After two weeks of journaling and self-inquiry, he realized he feared financial responsibility. Through Gateway meditations, he reframed money as *freedom.* Within months, he launched a side business and cleared his debt.

Scientific Insight: Gateway Process Validated

Declassified CIA documents show participants successfully engaged in remote viewing, time distortion, and "patterning" (manifestation through visualization). The neurological basis? Theta state integration—activating deep parts of the brain and heart coherence, which align with quantum field influence.

Quantum Perspective:

Grinberg's theory aligns with what modern physicists like David Bohm suggested—that the universe operates on a holographic model, where consciousness actively interacts with energy fields to shape experience.

You are not visualizing for fantasy—you are *communicating with the unified field.*

Sustaining Your Wealth Gateway — Daily, Weekly, Monthly

Mastery isn't a moment—it's a lifestyle. Here's how to keep your wealth frequency aligned long-term:

Daily:
- Wealth Gateway Ritual (see above).
- 3 affirmations spoken with emotion.
- Nightly journal: *"How did I show up today as the frequency of abundance?"*

Weekly:

- Set a 10-minute review session every Sunday.
- Ask:
  - What beliefs tried to resurface?
  - Where did I act from scarcity?
  - What did I manifest or attract?

Monthly:

- Create a *Wealth Frequency Vision Map*.
  - Photos, symbols, and words that represent your next level.
  - Update monthly based on progress and clarity.

Stay consistent. What you do *consistently* becomes your new default reality.

Final Reflection: you Are the Gateway

Let this be your closing truth:

> *You are not becoming abundant. You are remembering that you already are.*

The Gateway isn't outside of you. It's not at Langley or in the hands of monks or gurus. It is here. Now. In your breath. In your belief. In your inner world. This moment is the doorway.

Walk through it.

You've reclaimed your frequency.
You've rewritten your beliefs.
You've entered the field.

NOW LIVE AS IF YOUR WEALTH IS ALREADY HERE—BECAUSE IN THE QUANTUM REALM OF CONSCIOUSNESS...IT IS!

-The End-

Conclusion

As we reach the end of our journey together, it's important to pause and reflect on the transformative concepts we've explored. In this book, we've delved into the intricate relationship between energy, frequency, and wealth, uncovering a path towards financial empowerment that's as profound as it is accessible. The underpinning truth we've come to understand is that everything, including money, is a form of energy. The world around us vibrates with frequencies, and by learning to resonate with these vibrations, we can attract the wealth and abundance we desire into our lives.

This journey began with a foundational understanding: our thoughts, emotions, and beliefs are key elements in shaping our financial reality. By aligning these with positive frequencies, we open ourselves up to a realm of possibilities where prosperity flows naturally. We've explored how mindfulness practices can help in becoming more aware of our energetic states, enabling us to make conscious shifts towards harmonious living. Through energy healing techniques, we've learned to release blockages that hinder our ability to attract wealth, allowing for a free flow of abundance.

Applying these principles isn't limited to theoretical ideas; they can be woven seamlessly into daily life for meaningful change. For instance, incorporating meditation into your routine not only centers your mind but also tunes your personal vibration towards positivity and abundance. Simple practices like sound frequency exposure, specifically listening to music at 528 Hz—often referred to as the "Love Frequency"—can enhance your visualization exercises, creating a fertile space for your financial goals to manifest. These strategies, while seemingly simple, are powerful tools that equip you to actively participate in shaping your financial destiny.

It's crucial to remember that genuine transformation requires consistency. Drawing parallels to the art of maintaining a musical instrument, your financial alignment demands regular attention and adjustments. Just as a musician polishes their skills through steady practice, you too must engage persistently with the practices you've embraced throughout this book. Consistent effort will ensure that your mindset remains attuned to the frequency of wealth, empowering you to nurture lasting abundance.

Now, imagine closing these pages with a sense of purpose and eagerness to implement what you've learned. Reflect on the aspects of our journey together that have resonated with you. Have any of the practices or principles stood out? Consider setting an intention that allows these insights to take root in your daily life. Perhaps committing to meditate on your financial goals every morning for a month could serve as a starting point. Engage with the universe consciously, send out clear intentions, and remain open to the responses you receive.

In taking action, you're invited to recognize how each moment offers an opportunity for growth and connection. The knowledge acquired here is not just an intellectual exercise; it is a living philosophy meant to be applied and tested in your own experience. As you apply these principles, observe the shifts in your perception and the subtle changes in your external world. Witness how newfound clarity and focus can profoundly influence your approach to wealth and abundance.

Your journey doesn't end here. Rather, this conclusion marks a new chapter filled with potential and promise. Embrace the insights gained from our exploration, and carry them forward as guiding lights on your path. Engage with a community of like-minded individuals who share your vision for integrating metaphysical principles into financial practices. Share your experiences, learn from others, and continue to grow both personally and spiritually.

Remember, attracting wealth is not solely about material gain, but also about enriching your life holistically. It's about achieving balance and harmony within yourself and with the universe. Financial empowerment is one aspect of a larger journey toward self-realization and fulfillment. By cultivating a mindset that resonates with abundance, you contribute positively not only to your life but also to the collective energy of the world.

As you step forward with conviction, know that you're equipped with the tools necessary to manifest your dreams. Whether you're engaging in daily meditations, practicing gratitude, or fine-tuning your vibration through sound, every action holds the power to align you closer to the wealth frequency. Trust in the process, stay committed to your growth, and watch as the doors of opportunity open wide.

Thank you for embarking on this enlightening journey. May you continue to explore and deepen your understanding of the connections between energy, frequency, and wealth. Let this knowledge empower you to create a life rich in abundance, joy, and purpose. Remember, the potential for a prosperous future lies within you—embrace it wholeheartedly and let it guide you to realize your deepest aspirations.

I'd Love to Hear From You!

If *Resonate With Riches* sparked a shift in your mindset, offered you clarity, or helped you align with the abundance you've always deserved—your feedback would mean the world to me.

Your honest review not only supports my journey as an author, but it also helps fellow readers discover this book at the perfect moment in their own lives. Even just a few words can make a powerful difference.

Please take a minute to leave a review on Amazon or Goodreads.

It helps more than you know—and I read every single one with deep gratitude.

With heartfelt thanks,
Alden Gray

--------- The End ----------

Made in United States
Orlando, FL
29 April 2025